A BEGINNER'S GUIDE TO WINDOWS 10

CONTENTS

Book Description

Windows 10, the latest version of the world's most popular operating system for PCs from Microsoft, was released this year, making for arguably one of the biggest announcements in this domain in 2015. Microsoft has introduced a truckload of new features, as well as streamlined the design and made a much attempt at combining the OS with the Metro style.

Are you one of those people who is dying to know all about it? We make the task easier for you in this book! Instead of traversing through a dozen links in order to find about all that this operating system offers, and still miss out on one thing or the other, here we present you with a comprehensive beginner's guide to Windows 10. Whether you're a beginner who's looking to upgrade his/her system to Windows 10, or you're an expert who already has upgraded to Windows 10 and wants to know all about the new features and tips and tricks instead of discovering them through a trial-and-error basis, you will find what you're looking for here!

In this book you will learn about:

- The availability of Windows 10
- The new features that Windows 10 introduces, and how they work
- The features that have been removed from the OS with Windows 10
- Some things you should definitely know about Windows 10 before upgrading, to get the full picture
- Tips and tricks on how to use Windows 10 more effectively and easily.

We hope that after reading this book, you will know all that you want to know about the OS, and also some vital things which will both help you make an informed decision about upgrading to Windows 10, as well as the information you need on how to make the most out of this upgrade!

INTRODUCTION

Microsoft Windows is the most popular operating system for PCs available. The first version of the OS was introduced way back in 1985, and since then has seen a lot of different version with steady improvements. The latest offering from Microsoft after Windows 8.1 is Windows 10.

Windows 10 was launched on the 29th of July 2015. There are a couple of things about this version that has piped people's interest in it. Firstly, Windows 10 is free. You don't have to purchase a genuine version of the next Windows; you can just directly upgrade to it. It will remain free for one year, after which you'll be able to buy Windows 10 Home for $119 and Windows 10 Pro for $199.

Secondly, Windows 10 brings the good old Start menu back. Ever since the highly confusing and out-of-place Metro Style was introduced with Windows 8, users have been crying over the absence of the traditional Start menu, and Microsoft has listened to these complaints and brought it back with the latest installment of the OS. This shall be covered in greater detail later.

While Windows 10 seems to be more of an incremental upgrade aimed at making some sense out of combination of Metro style and the good old Windows for PC, it does come bundled with some new and exciting features as well. Likewise, some features have been omitted from the OS as well. Some new ways have also been introduced to do the same tasks as before, in order to provide more convenience and ease of use. There are also some tips and tricks which will provide you with information on how to use Windows 10 more effectively, and get the most out of the experience. Finally, there are some things about the OS that every user who is planning on getting the upgrade should know about.

All of these things have been covered in a suitable amount of detail. So if you're planning on upgrading your system but would like to know more about it, in order to make an informed decision, we have it all here for you! Regardless of whether you're a computer expert or a beginner, everything you need to know about Windows 10 is at your fingertips here. Hopefully, this will help you in making the right decision!

Happy reading!

PART 1: WINDOWS 10 FOR PC

CHAPTER 1: AVAILABILITY

Windows 10 was launched on the 29th of July 2015, and it is now available. If you are running Windows 7 or Windows 8.1, you can upgrade to Windows 10, and here's the best part: It's absolutely free! You can either upgrade your existing system to it or do a fresh install. If you previously reserved your free copy of Windows 10, you will be notified when the latest version of the operating system is ready to be installed.

One of the most interesting things of note that came alongside the Windows 10 announcement that people running pirated versions of Windows can also upgrade to Windows 10. So if you're running a pirated version of Windows 7 or later on your PC, you can upgrade to Windows 10 too! However, an important clarification that needs to be made here is that after upgrading, your Windows shall still remain pirated – that is, you will essentially be running a pirated version of Windows 10. Upgrading to Windows 10 does not give your operating system a genuine license if it didn't have on in the first place.

There is a total of eight versions of Windows 10. They are as follows:

- Windows 10 Home
- Windows 10 Pro
- Windows 10 Enterprise
- Windows 10 Enterprise 2015 LTSB
- Windows 10 Education
- Windows 10 Mobile
- Windows 10 Mobile Enterprise
- Windows 10 IoT Core

Windows 10 has been released with the basic aim of reaching out to as many as people as possible. This is why Windows 10 aims to provide pretty much the same experience irrespective of what device you're using. Windows 10 requires quite basic specifications to run. The minimum requirements are a 1GHz processor, 1GB RAM and 16GB of hard disk space. As you can see, these are pretty basic requirements that you can find on just about on any PC or laptop. Therefore, you don't exactly need to upgrade your system in order to run Windows 10.

CHAPTER 2: THE NEW THINGS

As expected, Windows 10 comes bundled with a truckload of new features. Apparently, according to Microsoft's executive Vice President of operating systems, Terry Myerson, Windows 10 was such a major breakthrough that the company decided to skip the expected name, which was Windows 9, and instead jumped straight to double digits. Ergo, Windows 10.

To do justice to this move, Windows 10 has a lot of never-seen-before features. Some of them were expected, some of them feature users had been fantasizing about for a long time, and some of them were pleasant surprises. Here are the main new features the latest operating system from Microsoft:

THE START MENU IS BACK!

Probably the most exciting and anticipated feature that Windows 10 introduced was the revival of the iconic Start menu from all the previous version of the OS, apart from Windows 8 and Windows 8.1. It's not quite the same, though; it has some changes and is even better now. It also has tiles popping up instead of the standard listed options when the Start button is clicked. The left column of the menu is similar to Windows 7. It has the username and picture on the top. Below it is the most frequently used apps on the system. And below those are four options: File Explorer (which is expandable), Settings, Power and All Apps.

The right column contains the live tiles similar to Windows 8's. You can create sections to group these apps, so for example, you can keep games in one section, apps like Weather, Mail, Calendar under another section named 'Life at a glance' (which happens to be a default section), or something else. Moreover, you can drag and drop tiles into the menu according to your preference and can even resize the apps to suit your style.

The color of the tiles adjusts accordingly to the system color that has been set. Another new feature in the Start menu is that there are two kinds of it. One is the standard Start menu, and the other is the full-screen Start menu. The full-screen start menu, upon being clicked, shows the live tiles appear on the screen much like the Start menu from Windows 8. On the left side, there are options to show all apps, Power settings, and most used apps. However, this full-screen start menu is a lot more streamlined than the ones from Windows 8 and 8.1 and seems more natural.

Overall, the revival of the Start menu is one of the best features that Windows 10 brings to the table and makes for a smoother and more familiar and convenient experience.

STREAMLINED DESIGN

One of the subtle yet great features in Windows 10 is the overall look and feel of the operating system; it's a lot more streamlined now. It actually looks like a complete and coherent system now. Unlike Windows 8, which was basically the Metro style and Windows 7 plastered together, and made for a very confusing layout. Moreover, Windows 8 and 8.1 were more oriented towards touch devices, making the experience on a PC with a standard mouse or trackpad very inconvenient and difficult. Windows 10 is much better, and it's not just because of the improvement of the Start menu. It's everything really, from the way the title bars have been subtly redesigned, to small design changes here and there that one notices as one uses the operating system more and more; the design language makes sense, and more importantly, is one. In other words, Windows 10 is how Windows 8 should have been.

MULTIPLE DESKTOPS

This isn't a particularly new feature if you've used Linux-based operating systems, but nevertheless it is a very welcome addition to Windows. If you haven't used Linux-based systems, then you're in for a treat. Windows 10 introduces the concept of or multiple desktops. Basically, the concept is that you can now have separate workspaces on your system. So for example, you can have work-related programs in one workspace, such as IDEs if you're coding, or Photoshop if you're designing etc., along with Google Chrome of your preferred browser for the occasional browsing to look up things. You can have Microsoft Word opened in another desktop along with another window for the browser, for example, for any documentation that you might be working on. Finally, you could have songs playing in the music player in yet another desktop. You can create desktops for different purposes, and close them once you're done. This makes for effective multitasking and makes the experience more enjoyable and professional too!

SEARCH BAR

One of the new and unanticipated features that Windows 10 brings is the search bar on the taskbar at the bottom. It is situated right next to the Start button, saying "Search the web and Windows", and makes for a huge convenience. You can click it to quickly search for anything on either your computer or online through Bing. When you type something in this search bar, it shows results from both your PC, if any, and suggests related search terms to search for on the internet. It comes in handy when you want to quickly look for something, either online or on your PC, and don't want to open up the desired program. Simply clicking on the search bar without typing anything opens Cortana, which shall be covered in detail later.

MICROSOFT EDGE

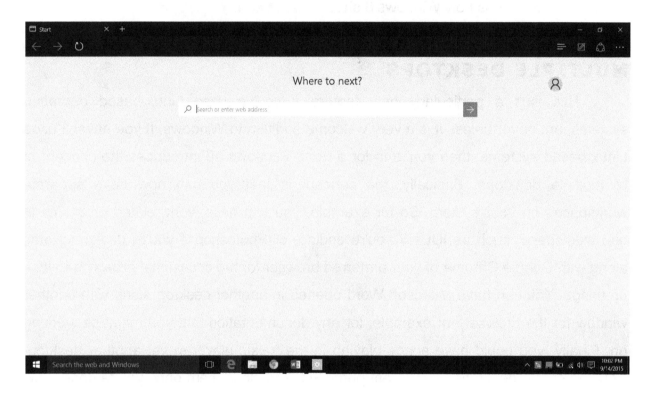

Another highly anticipated feature that Windows 10 ships with is the new browser. Microsoft has finally come up with a browser which can stand toe to toe with other popular browsers like Chrome and Firefox, the brand new Microsoft Edge. Microsoft Edge is in a lot of ways superior over its predecessor, and the most obvious way how is performance. Microsoft Edge is blazing fast. It opens immediately, which is in sharp contrast to how long Internet Explorer used to take to open. The browsing itself is a smoother and faster experience too; web pages load quickly, and the scrolling does not stutter or lag anymore. It's a great experience!

Furthermore, Microsoft Edge ships with some new and exciting features. For example, you can switch between light and dark themes. The light theme has shades of light grays, whereas the dark theme is full black. You can set what to see when you first open Edge: the MSN start page, the new tab page, previous pages, or a specific set of pages, or page. Similarly, you can also set what you want to see when you open a new tab.

Edge also allows you to draw on web pages. This is a very useful feature. You can draw something on web pages, choosing from a list of colors as you do so, or add a text box somewhere to type in something, or even highlight a piece of text. There is also an eraser to remove anything you might have added accidentally. You can also crop out a certain part of the web page. Once you're done making your additions, you can save the web page to OneNote, Favorites or add them to your Reading List, or share them with your friends.

Microsoft Edge also has some important security features that one should note. It offers InPrivate browsing, for one. When enabled, Edge will not store any browser information like cookies, history or any temporary files from the session. You also have features like popup blocking, SmartScreen Filter, and they Do Not Track request. Edge also allows you to choose you how you want to treat cookies.

QUICK ACCESS

The File Explorer in Windows 10 also sees a small upgrade, in the form of a new feature called Quick Access. It shows the most frequently accessed folders on the left sidebar. This is very useful if you're used to accessing a folder very frequently, and even more so if that particular folder is stowed away somewhere that requires a lot of navigation. In addition, the most recently accessed 20 items are also shown in the File Explorer when you open it. This is useful if there is some file you've been working on for some days, such as a document, or a PSD file. Some people find this feature annoying or useless, though. Quick Access can be turned off in the settings, though.

NOTIFICATIONS

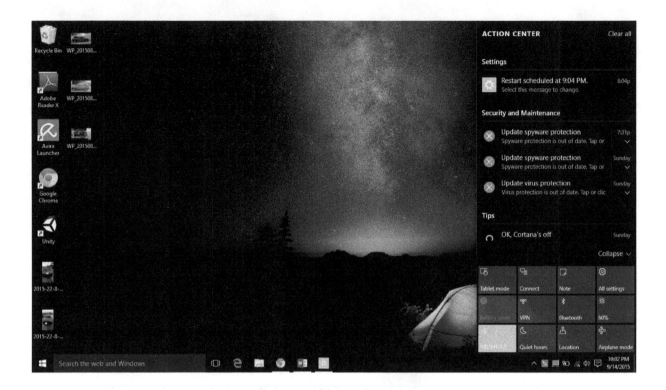

In an attempt to make the experience of using Windows 10 feel the same – or as similar as it can be – no matter what device you're using, Windows 10 introduces a notification tray in the version of the operating system for PCs. This notification tray, called Action Center, is exactly like the one in phones and tablets using Windows 10. It is situated on the extreme right of the taskbar, next to the time and date. It is shaped like a small message box, the kind you see in comics. Clicking on it reveals the Action Center, which displays all your notifications from the top.

The notifications are things like a system restart that needs to be scheduled for installing updates, antivirus or spyware protection being out of date, any mail that you may have received etc. They are also expandable, to provide more details. It also features quick setting toggles on the bottom – features that you can turn on and off by simply clicking on them – just like the toggles available on Windows Mobile.

The toggles are for settings like Wi-Fi, Airplane mode, Bluetooth, Battery Saver, All Settings etc. These toggles are a very handy feature since they allow you to get quick settings without cluttering the taskbar. By default, the total number of toggles displayed is 12, although you can collapse them to just four. Similarly, a Clear All option available can clear all notifications displayed in the Action Center, instead of clearing them away one by one.

ALL SETTINGS

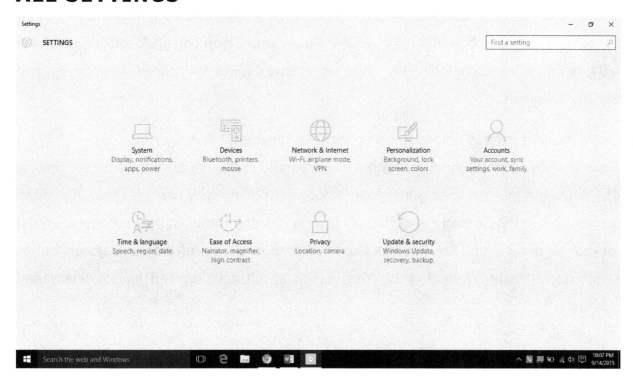

One of the most annoying things in previous versions of Windows was how almost every setting was in the Control Panel. So to change any aspect of your system, you had to dig through the plethora of options available in the Control Panel in the form of a list, find the option, and then dig through the sub-options that opened before you found what you were looking for. Moreover, the Control Panel was usually hidden, and locating it was quite an arduous process in itself.

Those days are gone now with the advent of Windows 10. To make things simplistic, easy and convenient, Windows 10 offers a simple 'All Settings' option in the Action Center, which is available as a toggle. Clicking on it brings up a clean window with big icons and simple descriptions. The icons and descriptions together help you narrow down whatever it is you're looking for under a single option.

However, if you're still confused and don't know what option whatever it is you're looking for should appear under, fear not. There is also a search bar on the top right of this window. It can allow you to search for any setting. So for example, if you're looking to change the amount of time your PC waits before going to sleep, you simply type in 'Power' in this search bar, and a list of options appear with matching keywords, ordered by relevance. The option at the top will be 'Power and Sleep settings', clicking on which will bring up what you're looking for: how much time it takes for your PC to go to sleep in various situations.

One important thing to note is that this does not mean that Windows 10 does not have a Control Panel. The Control Panel is still here, and pretty much the same as before. Thanks to the many conveniences that Windows 10 offers, you can avail one of them to quickly launch the Control Panel. Simply type in 'Control Panel' in the search bar on the taskbar to bring it up! So yes, the Control Panel is still here; the All Settings option simply provides an alternative way for you to reach your desired setting easily and quickly.

CONTINUUM

When Windows 8 was unveiled to the world, one of the biggest complaints that PC users registered after a few days of usage was how the new version of the operating system was more user friendly for devices with a touch display, rather than with a keyboard and mouse. It's true; snapping windows left and right, navigating through the new Start screen and so on was all tasks that were marginally easy to perform using a touch screen as compared to a mouse and keyboard.

With Windows 10, Microsoft aimed to resolve this issue, as well as live up to their promise of providing a unified experience on smartphones, tablets and PCs, by introducing a brand new and highly sensational feature: Continuum. The core concept of this feature is that the interface will adapt accordingly to the kind of system you're using. So for example, if you're using a touch interface, Windows 10 will show in the tablet mode, which is more touch friendly. If you're using a keyboard and mouse, Windows 10 will feature the desktop mode, which is easier to navigate using the aforementioned devices.

The true power of this feature comes into play when you're using a device, which is a combination of both touchscreen and a keyboard and mouse (like the Microsoft Surface). In such a case, Windows will seamlessly switch between layouts as per usage. So if you're using the touchscreen, Windows 10 will be in tablet mode, but as soon as you attach the keyboard and mouse, it will switch to desktop mode. This fluid transaction will help to reach out to a greater deal of users, who are still using desktops or are relying on touch or a combination of both.

SNAP ASSISTS

Window snapping was a feature that was first introduced in Windows 7. It allowed you to quickly snap any open window to the side without you having to drag it and resize it manually. It was a very handy feature since it allowed you to keep more than one app open in front of you, and allowing you to maximize the screen real estate of your PC.

With Windows 10, Microsoft has made sure that this feature not only stays but also becomes even more convenient and easy to use. There are more snap options now. You can drag a window by clicking and holding on its title bar and if you drag it to the left or right corner, an outline will appear. When you let go, the window will automatically adjust as so to take the corresponding half of the screen. If you drag a window to a corner and then let go, it will automatically adjust as so to take up a quarter of the screen.

You can also snap windows by using the arrow keys on the keyboard. Windows 10 comes with some very handy shortcuts for that which not only makes moving windows around easier, but also kind of fun! Pressing the Windows key + Up maximizes a windows, and Windows key + Down brings it to a smaller state. Windows key + Right will snap a window to the right half of the screen, and vice versa with Windows key + Left. If you want a make a windows fit across a quarter of the screen, first snap it to either the left or right half of the screen, and then press Windows key + Up to Windows key + Down to fit it across the specific quadrant. All of the snapping actions are very fast and fluid, making for a pleasurable viewing experience, so much so that in the first few days of using the operating system, you'll be snapping windows here and there just for fun!

Snap Assist is a feature which comes into play when you snap a window to the left or right, or when you have windows snapped to three-quarters. In other words, it comes up when you have either one-half or only one-quarter of the screen remaining. In such a case, the Snap Assist tool will bring up your remaining apps in the remaining portion of the screen in the form of thumbnails. You simply click on any one of them, and that window takes up the remaining portion of the screen.

THE IMPROVED COMMAND PROMPT

One particular aspect of the previous versions of Windows that was pretty stagnant was the Command Prompt. With each release, users would hope that they would introduce more features into the Command Prompt, and each time they would be disappointed. With Windows 10, it seems like Microsoft has finally received the complaints of their users related to the Command Prompt, and introduced some really sought after features.

Now, the Command Prompt isn't something a lot of people use. In fact, there might be many users out there who may not even know that the Command Prompt exists, or what its use is. While it is a bother using the Command Prompt at all, especially when the GUI (Graphical User Interface) of the Windows is amazing and allows you to perform all the actions you normally need to, there are quite a lot of people who use the Command Prompt. Most of these people are those who are used to the Linux environment and use its terminal frequently. For them, using the Command Prompt might even be preferable as compared to the good old mouse actions! Therefore, the following changes are very important to them.

Resizing. Up until Windows 8.1, the Command Prompt had very limited resizing capabilities. The length of the windows was adjustable from top to bottom, but the width was fixed and could not be increased beyond a certain limit. Similarly, you couldn't get a full-screen view of the Command Prompt. But now both features are available in Windows 10. And since it can be resized, it can also be snapped to a side or quarter.

Quick Edit. This feature allows you to select text on the Command Prompt as you would normally, like on a web page, a text file or as such. By default, this option was disabled, but in Windows 10 that isn't the case. Selecting text with your mouse intuitively just became even more mainstream. You can enable or disable this option by right-clicking on the title bar, and selecting Properties.

More options. By going into the Properties, you'll realize the new Command Prompt also offers some new options, along with the good old ones!

Ctrl key shortcuts. Out of all the various keyboard shortcuts that are available in Windows, or maybe even in all popular operating systems, which is the most widely used? 99% percent people will answer "Ctrl-C and Ctrl-V" without hesitation. The copy and paste features are ones we don't know what we would do without, and their keyboard shortcuts are just as convenient. However, this convenience wasn't available in the Command Prompt. With Windows 10, this issue finally got addressed too.

Opacity. You can now set the transparency of the Command Prompt as well. By going into Properties, you can drag the slider under the 'Colors' tab to change the transparency between 0 and 100%. This feature particularly comes in handy when you're using the Command Prompt and you have to type in an arduous filename that you just can't remember. Previously, you had to keep switching back and forth between the Command Prompt and the file explorer, to see the next letter of the file and type, and then back again. With transparency set to a suitable amount, you can see the contents of the background, and won't have to switch back and forth anymore.

SETTING KEYBOARD SHORTCUTS FOR PROGRAMS

In Windows 10, there is more than one way to open up a program. You can open it from the Start menu, you can open it from the desktop or the File Explorer, you can search for it from the search bar and then open it, or you can pin it to the taskbar and open it from there.

However, that isn't enough... Or so Microsoft thought. Especially for the keyboard-pro people who prefer to do every task with the keyboard and rely extremely heavily on keyboard shortcuts, Microsoft has provided a useful feature which prevents them from lifting their fingers from the keyboard and bringing them to the touchpad in order to open up a program. Now, you can define keyboard shortcuts for programs.

In all fairness, this feature was available in previous versions of Windows. But this has always been a very less-known feature, so if you didn't know about it before, here's how you go about it: Open the Properties of the program. Normally, this would mean that if it's a desktop app, you would have to locate it in the directory in which it is installed, which might result in a lot of searching – an easier way would be to go to the app from the Start menu, right-click it and select 'Open File Location'.

It would take you directly to the location where the program is installed. If the program you're looking to create a keyboard shortcut for is a Windows native app, then you would have to drag it from the Start menu onto the desktop first, in order to create a shortcut. In either case, once you have the program located in the File Explorer or desktop, right-click on it and select 'Properties'. Under the 'Shortcut' tab, you will find an option 'Shortcut key', with a text field to its right. Simply type in the combination of keys which you would like to serve as a keyboard shortcut for opening the application (such as Ctrl + Alt + Q), and then press 'Okay', or 'Apply'.

Congratulations, your new settings have been saved, and you can now open applications right from your keyboard, like a pro!

UNIVERSAL APPS

When Microsoft set out on their mission to provide a tight integration between the versions of their operating system running on phones, tablets and PCs, they weren't kidding. One of the biggest and most revolutionary features that Windows 10 introduces is something we've been hearing about for quite some time: universal apps.

The basic concept of universal apps is that applications need to be developed only once, and can then run on multiple platforms. So for example, if the Slack team wants to build an application of their program for Windows, they won't have to develop a separate version for PC, tablet and phone anymore. No, what will happen instead that they will build just one application, which will then run on Windows 10 regardless of whether it's on a PC, tablet or phone? How? To understand this, remember the concept of Continuum we mentioned earlier. Just like the operating system itself, applications will also be able to change layouts based on the nature of the device!

While this may not seem like a very important feature for the normal user, it is groundbreaking for the developers. As is quite a common knowledge, Windows currently has a very small number of applications in the app store, and this feature will certainly contribute a lot in attracting developers towards this platform – primarily because it means they'll have to develop the app only once and can then see it run on multiple platforms. Kudos to responsive design!

It is not only on PCs, tablets and smartphones that universal apps will run on. More devices are being added to the Windows family that will avail this feature, such as Xbox, HoloLens, and Surface Hub etc.

Another related and just as exciting announcement that Microsoft made while unveiling Windows 10 is that iOS and Android developers will now be able to port their apps and games directly to Windows 10. What it means is that developers won't have to fully redevelop their apps for Windows. The idea sounds simple enough; however, the execution is slightly more complex, as any developer could figure. Nevertheless, this is a groundbreaking announcement that will attract a lot of app developers towards the Windows platform and ultimately solve one of the biggest problems it faces: lack of apps in the app store. Microsoft has been testing their tools for this, and the Candy Crush Saga game that exists in the Windows Phone Store has in fact been converted from iOS code without any modifications!

CORTANA ON PC

When Apple unveiled Siri, the smart digital assistant on the iPhone, the world was awed. Siri certainly was a great feature on a smartphone. Google replied sometime later with their own digital assistant, Google Now. Google Now didn't have the personality that Siri did, but rather focused more on the tasks it was basically designed for. And then came Microsoft's reply: Cortana.

Cortana was unveiled with Windows Phone 8.1 and aimed to provide something that was a mix of Siri and Google Now, that is, had the both aspects of both. The personality of Siri, and the accuracy of Google Now. Now with Windows 10, Microsoft brings Cortana to PCs.

Using a digital voice assistant on a PC is slightly different than on a phone; for instance, speaking to your phone seems a lot more natural than speaking to your PC. You need an enabled microphone on your PC, and speaking to it might feel weird. But it can be great once you get the hang of it since it will provide a lot of useful features and hacks! For example, you can avail the use of her natural language abilities for search – provide filters! You can give her basic commands like "Find pictures from December", or tell her to open an application installed in your PC, or getting her to play music etc. If you do plan on speaking to her, make sure it's in a quiet place, with not a lot of background noise, otherwise that will mess up her voice recognition. Moreover, you will need to have a decent microphone in your PC. Finally, speech recognition works as good as the amount of training data provided, so the more you interact with her, the better she'll get at understanding you.

However, Microsoft has you covered as they provide the same option on PCs of speaking or typing your query into the text box as with Cortana on phones if you're not comfortable speaking to your PC or laptop. Opening Cortana presents you with a view of your daily dose of updates: news of any sports teams you follow, any major headlines, the weather etc. Also, Cortana can be activated without having to use the mouse or keyboard. You can simply say, "Hey, Cortana" to activate the digital voice, assistant! You can also provide her with your name, in order to tell her what to call you.

Other than that, Cortana comes with a bunch of interesting and useful features that proves that she's more than just a voice-based search engine. For instance, Cortana's Trip Planner can tell you how long it will take for you to reach your desired destination, how long it will take to get to the airport etc. You can also set reminders on Cortana. This is a very useful feature and users will be glad that they now have such a functionality available on PCs, to be able to set reminders easily.

Previously, as you might have noticed, people used to have a lot of sticky notes on their desktop with various notes inscribed on them in order to remind themselves of things they had to do. With Windows 10, Cortana takes care of that for you. Cortana can also give you reminders based on your location – location based reminders, as the technical term goes. Using maps, Cortana figures out your current location. So for example, if you set up a reminder like, "Remind me to call my wife when I'm at (some location)", it will remind you once your reach that location. Pretty handy, especially if you're in the habit of traveling and taking your laptop or tablet with you to work on the way!

When we mentioned that Cortana has a personality as well, it was true. Cortana can give you witty retorts to questions, and can even tell you a joke or sing you a song if you ask her to!

Apart from these, Cortana has a handful of other useful features and amusing things about her, but those are for you to discover. Go talk to her, and find out!

THE NATIVE APPS

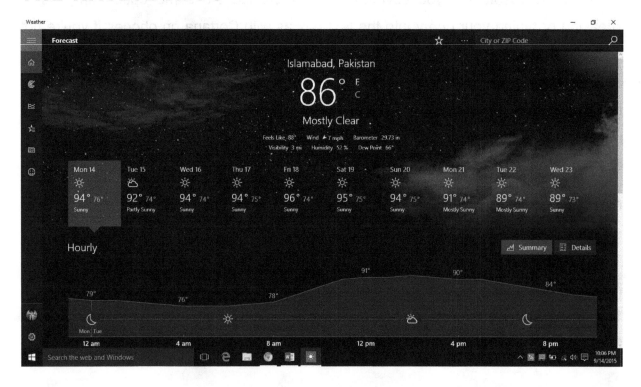

Windows 10 comes bundled with a bunch of native apps, such as Calendar, Mail, Weather etc., and they are an absolute delight to use! They are fast, fluid and the design has been overhauled, which means that not only are they more beautiful now, but also more coherent with the overall design language of the operating system, and a lot more mouse-friendly too. Many apps have ditched a horizontal layout in favor a vertical one, in order to avail use of the scrollbar.

The Store looks better too, with the apps laid out in a more organized and sorted manner, making it easier for you to find whatever it is you're looking for, and an overall simpler feel. Most people never used the native apps on Windows 8 and 8.1 for PC, but Windows 10 provides a compelling reason to try them out and stick to using them!

CHAPTER 3: THE MISSING THINGS

While Microsoft is introducing a slew of new features with Windows 10, each more exciting than the last, there are some features it is getting rid of. Obviously, an upgrade doesn't just mean the introduction of new features; it also means dispatching of some unpopular, unwanted features from the operating system. Microsoft has tried to remove mostly those features from their latest offering which were either of no use anymore, or those for which newer (and perhaps better) replacements are being introduced.

Of course, just how useful or irrelevant any feature is to an operating system depends on a lot upon individual perception. What if one may find useless may be perceived by another as something he can't live without. However, the opinion of the majority certainly matters in such a scenario, and here are the features that Windows 10 has gotten rid of. Will you miss them?

WINDOWS MEDIA CENTER

To be fair, the Windows Media Center was something the majority of people never used. In fact, there were many people who didn't even know about it! The all-in-one entertainment hub that Microsoft provided in previous versions of the OS has finally been removed. Now, Microsoft has instead offered several native-media playing apps which are not grouped together in a 'Center'. For example, there is the Photos app for viewing pictures, Groove Music for playing your songs etc. The Windows Media Center isn't something that a lot of people will greatly miss, which is why this is probably a very smart move on Microsoft's part.

WINDOWS 10 HAS NO HEARTS

By this statement, we do not mean that Windows 10 is a cold, heartless operating system (although technically, it kind of is, despite the strong case that Cortana's lively personality puts up). Remember Hearts? The card game in all previous versions of Microsoft's operating system that everyone loved and grew up playing?

Well, if you install Windows 10, you won't be able to relive those memories, and your children won't be able to play the same card game growing up as you did.

DESKTOP GADGETS

Desktop Gadgets were introduced in Windows 7. The chances are that you might not be familiar with them, or if you are, you didn't use them a lot. They were a lot like the widgets that you can place on the home screen on Android. Small graphical objects like a clock, or a calendar that you could place on the desktop. Windows 10 has removed that concept altogether. There are no desktop gadgets in the latest from Microsoft.

FLOPPY DISCS

In the technologically advanced and extremely fast-paced world we live in today, we are introduced to new technologies every other day, which leaves the tech freaks and geeks amongst us breathless with excitement. However, every time we are introduced to a new piece of technology, it inadvertently signals the end of an old one.

When CDs arrived, they signaled the end of floppies. The end of CDs was marked by DVDs, and the end of DVDs by USBs. Windows 10 has removed support for the lowest member of this food chain: floppies. You will have to install new drivers in order to enable floppy support on Windows 10, although why anyone would use floppies in this day and age is incomprehensible.

DVDS

What is more surprising than the above-mentioned point is the fact that Microsoft has with Windows 10, also withdrawn support for DVDs. Anyone who watches DVDs on their PC or laptop is in for a shock, although there may not be many such people left in today's day and age. Nevertheless, not all hope is lost; people who do want to watch DVDs on Windows 10 can do so by installing third-party software, such as VLC Player.

CHAPTER 4: TIPS AND TRICKS

After learning about the new features of a new operating system, you might feel that's enough for you to get started. And in most cases, it actually is. But sometimes, it is helpful to be aware of a few tips and tricks that could help you along the way.

As far as Windows 10 is concerned, Microsoft claims that it's 'the best one yet', and it's hard to argue. With Windows 10, Microsoft has finally bridged the gap between PCs and the Metro style they've been trying to incorporate for quite some time. It has also provided us with some very exciting features such as Continuum and Universal Apps, which make for a very exciting future, one that we certainly look forward to! There were some people, who had taken to claiming that Microsoft is a dying beast, and with the dominance of Android and iOS, Windows won't survive for long, but with Windows 10, Microsoft has made quite the comeback!

After going through all the new features that Windows 10 is providing, the chances are that you can't wait to try out this new operating system, and get to exploring it for yourself. While we can't blame you for that, and hope that you'll have a great experience, there are a few tips and tricks that you should have up your sleeve. They'll only improve your experience of using the latest and best that Microsoft has to offer, and they will also help you guide yourself out of trouble should you get into any.

BOOTING INTO SAFE MODE

If someone runs into a major problem while using their PC, safe mode is a troubleshooting mode that people usually boot into. It is a mode where all the unnecessary drivers and programs have been disabled and helps you locate the source of the problem. While the use of such drastic measures is usually felt only while encountering a big problem (read: do not boot into safe mode if your Wi-Fi disconnects or something), it is helpful to know how exactly to boot into Safe mode should the need arrive.

Unlike the earlier versions of Windows, booting into Safe mode is quite easy in Windows 10, and doesn't involve anything arduous or complicated. And no, there's no need for opening up a Command Prompt! Basically, what you need to do is to enable Startup Settings when you turn on your PC, and it is from there that you can boot into Safe mode.

To enable Startup Settings, open the All Settings menu from the Action Center, and then select the 'Update and Recovery' option. Once that opens up, go to 'Recovery', and then 'Advanced Startup'. Once you do this, your PC will restart in recovery mode. You will be met by a light blue screen with three options, and it is from here that you can enable Startup Settings. The three options will be: 'Continue', 'Troubleshoot', and 'Turn off your PC'. Select 'Troubleshoot'. In the menu that follows, select 'Advanced Options'. Now you will be met with a series of different options, one of which shall be 'Startup Settings'. Bingo. Click on this option to enable it. You will be met with a list of things that will be changed upon restart, and a 'Restart' button. Click it to restart your system.

When your system boots up, you'll see a blue screen with the Startup Settings on it. You can choose any option with your keyboard. You can press Enter if you want to boot manually. Otherwise, press F4 or 4 to boot into Safe Mode, F5 or 5 to boot into Safe Mode with networking, and F6 or 6 to boot into Safe Mode with the Command Prompt.

SHARING FILES QUICKLY

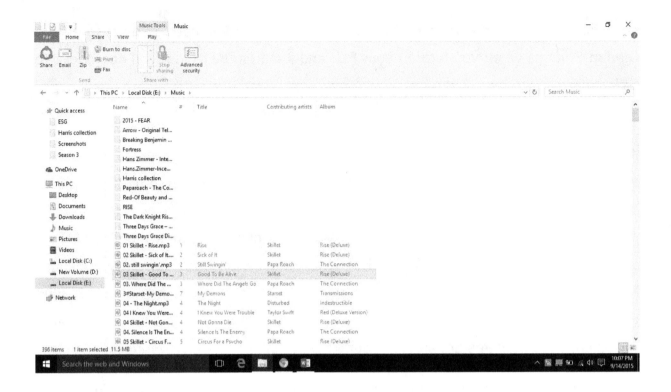

Suppose you're going through your photos stored in your hard disk. They are photos from the days of your university, and viewing them has made you very nostalgic. You come across a particular photo which reminds you of some event at your university, and seeing all your friends in this picture makes you miss them and want to share this with them. All of a sudden you remember that it's Thursday, and, therefore, you can avail the 'Throwback Thursday' concept to upload this picture on Facebook and jog your friends' memories as well!

Now, normally to carry out such an action, you would have to open Facebook, either in your browser or the official application available on the Windows Store and share the picture from there. However, Windows 10 comes with a small but very useful feature that allows you to share picture directly! Here's what you have to do:

Locate the item you want to share in the File Explorer, and select it. Then in the menu bar above, select the 'Share' tab. On the extreme left, you'll see an option 'Share'. When you click it, a sidebar will open on the left along with a list of applications through which you can share the file. Select the application you want to share the file through, and you're good to go! The applications that appear on the sidebar depends on the type of file that you're trying to share. For example, if you're trying to share a photo, both Facebook and Mail will appear, but if you're trying to share a zipped file, only Mail will appear.

You can also change the apps that show on the sidebar when you decide to share a file. To do this, go to All Settings, select System and then the 'Share' tab. Here, you will be presented with a list of applications through which you can share files, and you can toggle them on or off.

MOVING APPS BETWEEN DESKTOPS

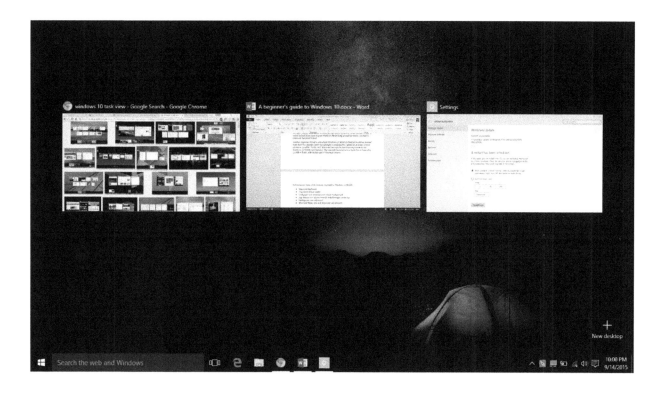

The addition of virtual desktops in Windows 10 presents an exciting opportunity, especially for those people who use their PCs as workstations, or generally any person who at any point in time has a lot of applications open and wants to organize his apps. However, multiple desktops are something that will take a certain amount of time to get used to. In order to make handling them easy, and utilizing them to their full potential, here's a nifty feature you should be aware of: moving open apps between desktops.

In order to move an application from one desktop to another, open up the Task View. The Task View trigger is located on the taskbar, right next to the search bar. Clicking on it will reveal all your open programs, in the form of thumbnails, the size of which will adjust according to the number of programs that are open. More apps = smaller size of thumbnails. Once you open the Task View, you will see thumbnails for your open desktops at the bottom as well, if you have more than one desktop open. You will also see a plus sign with 'New Desktop' at the bottom right corner of the screen. Clicking on it will add another virtual desktop. You can simply click and drag an application thumbnail onto one of the open desktops below, and letting go will move that application in the specific desktop.

You can also drag an app onto the 'New Desktop' sign and let go, upon which the app will be added to a new desktop. Another thing to note is that if you have two desktops open, and you close one of them through the Task View, all the apps in the close desktop will move to the other one. Therefore, closing a desktop does not mean that all its applications will close as well!

KEYBOARD SHORTCUTS

Of course, no guide to an operating system is complete without some handy keyboard shortcuts. They make our lives so much easier and faster, especially for those people who code or write for a living. Actions such as copying, cutting or pasting text, switching between applications, opening up File Explorer etc., are made infinitely easier and more convenient with the help of keyboard shortcuts.

The keyboard shortcuts that Windows 10 introduces are as follows:

Windows key + Right: snap a window to the right half of the screen

Windows key + Left: snap a window to the left half of the screen

Windows key + Up while windows is in left or right half: snap window to upper quarter of screen

Windows key + Down while windows is in left or right half: snap window to lower quarter of screen

Windows key + Up: Maximize window

Windows key + Down: Minimize window

Windows key + Tab: Task View

Windows key + Ctrl + D: Create new desktop

Windows key + Ctrl + Right: Move to next desktop

Windows key + Ctrl + Left: Move to the previous desktop

Windows key + Ctrl + F4: Close current desktop

CHAPTER 5: THE THINGS YOU SHOULD KNOW

Windows 10 is generally considered to be a massively refined and improved version of Windows 8 and 8.1. The latest from Microsoft is fast, snappy, is a lot more coherent in terms of design language, and comes bundled with a set of neat features. However, there are some things that you should know about Windows 10, which are generally considered the sort of annoying by most of the people. Since this is a complete guide to Windows 10, the following 'features' are things you should know about the operating system, and what you can do about them should you want to change them!

UPDATES

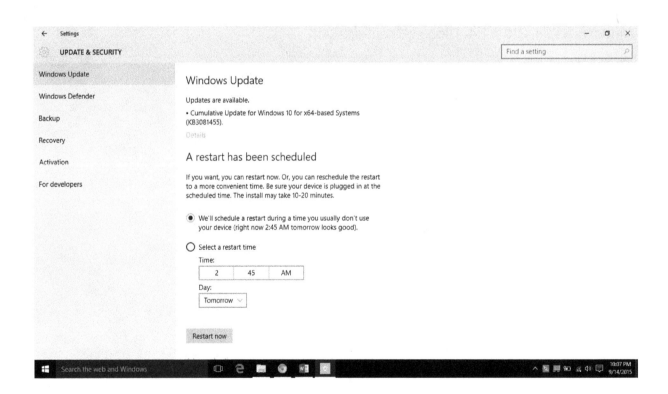

Windows 10, like its predecessors, downloads updates to your PC. However, the catch here is that you can't turn automatic updates off. Windows 10 will download updates to your PC whenever they're available, and often it squeezes your bandwidth while doing so. This is quite annoying, and you can't turn off updates unless you turn off the update service altogether from the Task Manager.

Moreover, by default Windows 10 is set to restart your PC automatically in order to install your updates. So it's very much possible that you're working some important project, and Windows will abruptly restart your PC to finish installing updates before you could even save your work! Not only is this annoying, but it might even cut across you working on something very important. However, this is something you can change, and you should. You can schedule your restarts, to a time that suits you, such as when you're not working.

To do this, go to All Settings, Update and Recovery, Windows Update, and then Advanced Options. On the top, you'll notice a drop-down list under 'Choose how updates are installed'. In this drop-down menu, the option 'Automatic (recommended)' would be selected by default. Select it and change it to 'Notify to schedule restart'. Now every time Windows needs to undergo a restart in order to install updates, it will notify, and you can choose a time that suits you.

TURNING OFF NOTIFICATIONS

The Action Center on Windows displays notifications much like on your phone. It is one of the features on the PC version of Windows 10 which unifies the whole experience and makes it feel like you're using one system across all devices. However, getting notifications on your PC much like your smartphone might get kind of annoying. Especially if you're in the middle of some work, the constant notifications will create quite a disturbance.

Or if you're showing your work to your boss and your notifications start showing up one after the other, well that would be kind of embarrassing. For these reasons or any else, if you want to turn off notifications on your PC, here's how you can do so: Go to All Settings, System, Notifications, and Actions.

From here, you can simply toggle which kind of notifications you would like to receive, and which you don't. Similarly, you can also set which apps can display notifications, and which apps can't. So for example, you might want to receive updates from your Antivirus program and Mail client on but may want to disable them from Windows Feedback.

SETTING DEFAULT APPS

While Microsoft Edge is a massive improvement over Internet Explorer, and not only is a web browser you can use, but might also want to, the fact remains that by now, many people are hooked to Google Chrome or Mozilla Firefox too much, and they can't let them go – for now, at least. Similarly, while the Photos app that comes bundled with Windows 10 is great, it's not quite the same as Picasa. In these cases or others, you might want to change the default apps for various actions to others of your preference. You can change most default apps by going to All Settings, System, Default Apps. Here, you'll see the default apps set for various programs such as Maps, Music Player, and Web Browser etc. Click on a selected app, and a drop-down list will appear containing all apps on the PC which can open the specified program. Select the one you want, and voila! The default app for the selected program is now the one to your liking.

REMOVE THE SEARCH BAR

The search bar present on the taskbar is a handy way of quickly looking up some file on your computer, or searching the web for something without having to open the browser. However, it does present an unfamiliar look, and people who preferred the clean, uncluttered taskbar from Windows 8 and 8.1 will be disappointed. However, not to worry, you can remove the search bar if you want. Right, click on it to show a menu. Hover over the 'Search' option, which will present you with a sub-menu showing the following options: Hidden, Show search icon, Show search box.

Selecting the first option will remove the search bar from your taskbar altogether. However, if you want the search bar and the functionality of quick search that comes with it to remain, but not to take up too much space, you can select the 'Show search icon' option. Now instead of a whole search bar, you will have a small icon on your taskbar with a magnifying glass on it, signifying search. Clicking on it will present you with the same options that appear when you clicked on the search bar.

WINDOWS 10 CAN CATCH AND DISABLE PIRATED GAMES

While Windows 10 comes with a truckload of new features most of which are very exciting, there are some which make pause and reconsider upgrading to the latest version of the world's most popular operating system for PCs. One of these features is that Windows 10 can now monitor your system to catch and disable pirated games in your system.

The clause can be found in the user license agreement and goes thus:

"We may automatically check your version of the software and download software updates or configuration changes, including those that prevent you from accessing the Services, playing counterfeit games, or using unauthorized hardware peripheral devices. You may also be required to update the software to continue using the Services."

So yes, Windows 10 can prevent you from playing pirated games in your PC. The term 'unauthorized hardware peripheral devices' is ambiguous as to what it refers to. Nevertheless, hardcore gamers who use pirated games may want to think twice before upgrading to Windows 10. So far, this refers only to pirated games, not third party pirated software. It is also unclear what Microsoft exactly plans to do with this information. Will they simply disable pirated games, or will they pass on the information to law enforcement.

PART 2: WINDOWS 10 FOR SMARTPHONES

CHAPTER 6: WINDOWS 10 MOBILE

PCs aren't the only ones which are getting the Windows 10 update. The next upgrade for Windows Phones is Windows 10 Mobile. In order to provide a unified experience across all devices, Microsoft is pushing their latest version of the OS to their smartphones too.

Windows Phones have never been very strong in the smartphone market, and despite their efforts, that market has remained strongly dominated by Android and iOS. In what could be considered a last ditch effort to make a noticeable impact, Windows is using the biggest weapon in their arsenal: their dominance in the PC operating system market.

With Windows 10, Microsoft aims at bridging the gap between your smartphone and your PC. With concepts like Continuum and Universal Apps, your PC and smartphone will feel like one, and you won't constantly have to switch back and forth between the two devices. Moreover, Windows 10 Mobile introduces a couple of new exciting features as well which will make the experience better. These features are a combination of some things that the OS should've had from the start, and the competition has had for a long time, as well as some new innovative features which can help Windows 10 Mobile stand its own against the giants of the industry.

Windows 10 has not been released yet. Neither has it been given an official release date. Microsoft has been relatively quiet on that front. However, Microsoft launched the Insider program a few months back, signing up for which allows users to update their phones to the latest builds as they get released. Another purpose of the Insider program is for users to test the latest build on their phones and give feedback, which the developers will fix in the next release.

However, builds are not final versions; they're more of an experimental release; and generally contain bugs which could either be minor or major. The bugs are removed and features are added in the next build, and so on. If you use your Windows Phone as a daily driver, it is not recommended to sign up for the Insider program, since a build could have a major bug that could render your phone unusable from a certain perspective (such as Wi-Fi connection issues, camera is not working, apps force closing etc.).

If you really want to be in the know-how of the latest from Windows 10 Phone and can't resist waiting for the official release, be prepared for bug fixes ranging from minor to rendering the phone unusable, on the intensity scale. It would be best if you have a spare Windows Phone lying around the house; use that to check out the latest builds!

Another important thing to note about Windows 10 Mobile is that Microsoft has learned from their last mistake and is now pledged to pushing this update for as many of their phones as possible. To this end, Microsoft has kept the hardware requirements for Windows 10 Mobile very baseline. The smartphone must have a resolution of 800x480, 512MB of RAM, 4GB storage and a VGA back camera.

Following are some of the features expected in Windows 10 Mobile:

- Improved keyboard
- Improved Action Center
- Wallpaper now stretched over the whole background
- App drawer now shows recently installed apps on the top
- Settings are now organized
- Microsoft Edge, new and improved web browser.

CONCLUSION

So there you have it, folks! The new, the missing, the ugly about Windows 10, the latest version of the iconic operating system from Microsoft, as well as a few tips and tricks to make the most out of the great experience!

Our take? Windows 10 is a worthy upgrade for your system. The streamlined design gives the OS a coherent feel, the good old Start menu is back, and it comes with a set of cool new features that makes using it even more fun and effective. Moreover, Windows 10 is smooth, fast and snappy. Little transitions have been added to actions, so everything just doesn't sort of happen; you actually see it happening. The transitions are paced well enough, so that you do notice it, but they're not slow enough to be frustrating. Moreover, Windows 10 seems to be the a big step towards the future, with features like Continuum and Universal Apps ripe for the picking on the horizon!

However, if you are a person who relies heavily on pirated games and can't do without them, then you might want to give it a second thought since Windows 10 can disable pirated games. Maybe wait a bit to see what Microsoft actually does about it. Likewise, if good bandwidth is of the utmost importance to you and you can't afford the update service hogging it every time an update is available, then maybe you should hesitate. You could, of course, turn off the update service off altogether!

If the above two issues aren't a major problem for you, however, then we would strongly recommend getting the upgrade. Windows 10 is a solid effort by Microsoft, and it's worth it. Plus, it's free for a year, so why not give it a shot? If you don't like it, you can always downgrade to Windows 8 or 7.